What can I ...?

Feel

Sue Barraclough

Heinemann

Little Nippers

www.heinemann.co.uk/library
Visit our website to find out more information about **Heinemann Library** books.

To order:
☎ Phone 44 (0) 1865 888066
📄 Send a fax to 44 (0) 1865 314091
💻 Visit the Heinemann Bookshop at www.heinemann.co.uk/library to browse our catalogue and order online.

First published in Great Britain by Heinemann Library, Halley Court, Jordan Hill, Oxford OX2 8EJ, part of Harcourt Education. Heinemann is a registered trademark of Harcourt Education Ltd.

Editorial: Sarah Shannon and Louise Galpine
Design: Jo Hinton-Malivoire and Tokay,
  Bicester, UK (www.tokay.co.uk)
Picture Research: Melissa Allison
Production: Camilla Smith

Originated by Chroma Graphics (Overseas) Pte Ltd.
Printed and bound in China by South China Printing Company

ISBN 0 431 02205 4 (hardback)
09 08 07 06 05
10 9 8 7 6 5 4 3 2 1

ISBN 0 431 02211 9 (paperback)
09 08 07 06 05
10 9 8 7 6 5 4 3 2 1

British Library Cataloguing in Publication Data
Barraclough, Sue
What can I? – Feel
612.8'8
A full catalogue record for this book is available from the British Library.

Acknowledgements
The Publishers would like to thank the following for permission to reproduce photographs:
Alamy pp. **14-15**, **19** right, **19** top left, **22-23** (CLEO Photo); Bubbles p. **13** bottom; Corbis p. **15** all images; Digital Vision pp. **20-21**; Harcourt Education / Tudor Photography pp. **4-5**, **6**, **7**, **8**, **9**, **11**, **16**, **17**; Harcourt Education pp.**12**, **13** top, **18** (Gareth Boden); Getty Images / PhotoDisc p. **19** bottom; PhotEdit Inc. p. **10**.

Cover photograph reproduced with permission of Harcourt Education / Tudor Photography.

Every effort has been made to contact copyright holders of any material reproduced in this book. Any omissions will be rectified in subsequent printings if notice is given to the Publishers.

Contents

Wide awake 4

Warm clothes 6

Feels sticky! 8

Warm and dry 10

Squelch! Splash! 12

How does it feel? 14

Swinging and sliding 16

Hot and cold 18

Bathtime bubbles 20

Goodnight hugs 22

Index 24

Wide awake

Bed feels snug, but it is time to get up.

Briiii

Fluffy slippers feel **soft** on your feet.

Briiiing!

5

Warm clothes

A soft, woolly jumper will make you feel warm on cold mornings.

What are your favourite **warm** clothes?

Feels sticky!

Strawberry jam feels **sticky** on your tongue...

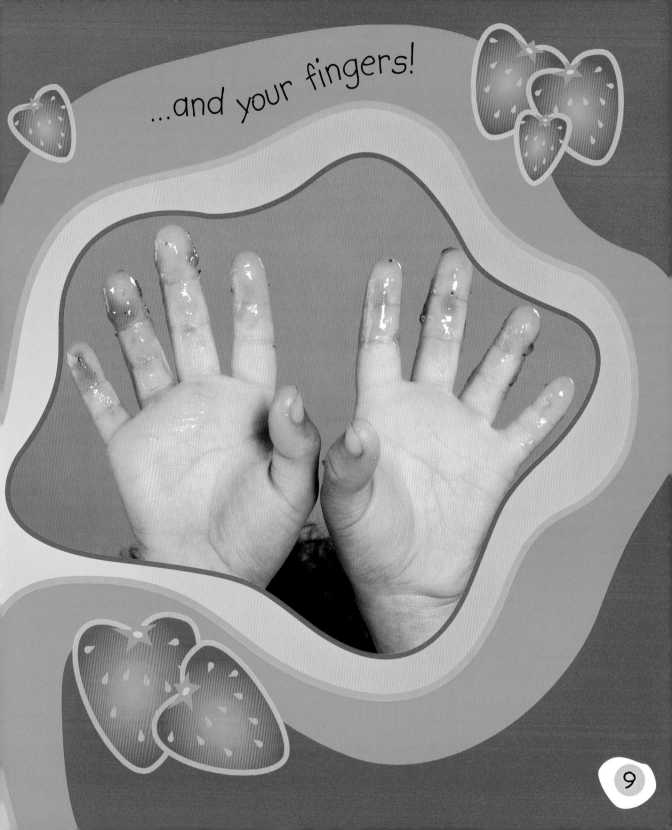

...and your fingers!

9

Warm and dry

Washing with warm water feels good.

Feel the water first. Make sure it's not too hot!

Fluffy towels feel soft against your skin.

How do each of these things **feel**?

squelch!

splash!

How does it feel?

These shells would feel **rough** to touch.

How would each thing **feel**?

prickly

soft

spiky

15

Swinging and sliding

Whoosh!

The wind **blows** on your face when you swing.

The slide feels **slippery** and **smooth**.

Swoosh!

Hot and cold

Holding a **hot** drink makes your hands feel warm.

Ice cream feels **cold** on your tongue.

Which things are **cold**?

Which things are **hot**?

Bathtime bubbles

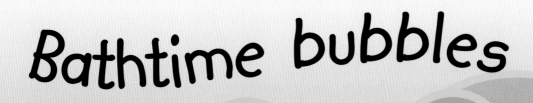

Bubbles are fun at bathtime!

Hee, hee!

They **tickle** your skin!

Goodnight hugs

A **cosy** bed feels
good at bedtime.

So do goodnight hugs!

23

Index

bed 4, 5, 22, 23

cold 6, 18, 19

slippers 4, 5

smooth 17

soft 6, 11

sticky 8, 9

tickle 20, 21

Notes for adults

This series encourages children to explore their environment to gain knowledge and understanding of the things they can see, smell, hear, taste, and feel. The following Early Learning Goals are relevant to the series:

• use the senses to explore and learn about the world around them
• respond to experiences and describe, express, and communicate ideas
• make connections between new information and what they already know
• ask questions about why things happen and how things work
• discover their local environment and talk about likes and dislikes.

The following additional information may be of interest
The skin has sensitive nerve endings that pick up information about texture, pressure, temperature, and pain, and send information to the brain to be processed.

Follow-up activities
Make a simple 'touchy-feely' box or bag to find out if children can identify objects by touch alone. Focussing on a specific sense helps children to use that sense more actively in their investigations. Create collages to explore textures and patterns.